Table of Contents

Table of Contents

Gluten-Free Desserts

Warning: While we make every attempt to write our recipes for gluten-free ingredients, many ingredients can vary by manufacturer. You must be careful to read labels and warnings, and stay aware of changing regulations regarding labeling. The safest way to eat gluten-free is by using fresh ingredients. Second, look for the certified gluten-free label. Third, call the manufacturer yourself to ask if the product is gluten-free, and produced in a designated gluten-free facility. Even if gluten products are not listed in the ingredients, it is possible to pick up airborne flour, for example, in a facility that is not dedicated gluten-free. Wheat-free is not the same as gluten-free. For example, modified corn starch, barley, and oats may contain gluten. Products you may not think of containing gluten may in fact contain gluten. A few of these include: spices such as cinnamon and cumin; canned goods such as broth and soup; sauces and salad dressings. The bottom line is to be vigilant about checking labels, and consulting the manufacturer when in doubt.

Whether you or a loved one must avoid gluten for medical reasons, or you've realized how much better you feel living gluten free, the recipes in this collection will soon become some of your best-loved dishes. You'll find that creating gluten free meals, side dishes and desserts for family and friends doesn't need to be intimidating. In fact, the recipes in this book make cooking gluten free as easy as 1-2-3. These recipes are so satisfying and stress-free you'll never miss the gluten. You'll find many healthy alternatives to the comfort foods we crave, and along the way you might just discover brand new family favorites.

ALMOND POUND CAKE

Ingredients:
1 1/2 cups gluten free flour mix
2 1/2 tsp baking powder
3/4 cups (1 1/2 sticks) unsalted butter, softened
1 1/2 cups granulated sugar
3/4 cup whole milk ricotta cheese
3/4 cup mascarpone cheese
1 tsp vanilla extract
1/2 tsp almond extract
3 eggs
Powdered sugar (optional)

Directions:
Preheat oven to 350 degrees. Spray a Bundt pan with non-stick cooking spray. In a small bowl, mix together flour and baking powder. Set Aside. Using an electric mixer, beat butter until light and fluffy. Add the sugar, ricotta, mascarpone, and vanilla. Continue to beat. Add eggs, one at a time, beating well after each addition. With mixer on low, add dry ingredients. Mix until just combined. Pour batter into prepared pan. Bake for 50 minutes to 1 hour – until a toothpick inserted in the center comes out clean. Invert onto a wire rack to cool. Sift powdered sugar over the top when cooled, if desired.

SWEET CHERRY CAKE

Ingredients:
1 can gluten free cherry pie filling
1 tsp almond extract
3/4 cup canola oil
1 1/2 cups sugar
1/3 cup milk
1 tsp vanilla
3 eggs
3 cups gluten free flour mix
2 tsp baking powder
1/4 cup cinnamon sugar

Directions:
Preheat the oven to 350 degrees. Spray a 9 x 13-inch cake pan with non-stick cooking spray. Open the can of cherries and stir in the almond extract. Set aside. In a large mixing bowl, combine the oil, sugar, milk, vanilla and eggs. Blend well. Add in the flour mix and baking powder, stirring to combine. Pour half the batter into the pan then spoon the cherry pie filling over the top. Spread remaining batter over the cherries and sprinkle cinnamon sugar on top. Bake for 15 minutes then turn oven down to 325 degrees and continue baking for 30 to 40 minutes.

LEMON CREAM CAKE

Cake Ingredients:
1 box gluten free yellow cake mix
1 cup whole milk
3 eggs
3/4 cup (1 1/2 sticks) butter, melted
1 tsp vanilla

Filling Ingredients:
1 lemon, juiced
1/2 cup heavy cream,
1/2 cup mascarpone cheese
1/2 cup powdered sugar

Crumb Topping Ingredients:
4 Tbsp butter, melted
3/4 cup of a gluten free lemon cake mix

Directions:
Preheat oven to 350 degrees. Spray two cake pans with non-stick cooking spray. Using an electric mixer, combine the cake mix, milk, eggs, butter, and vanilla. Pour batter into the prepared cake pans and bake for 25 minutes or until a toothpick inserted in the center comes out clean. Remove from oven and invert onto cooling rack. While the cake cools, make the crumb topping and filling.

For the topping, stir together the 4 Tbsp melted butter and 3/4 cup lemon cake mix until crumbly and set aside.

For the filling, combine the lemon juice, cream, mascarpone, and powdered sugar until smooth.

When the cake is cool, place one layer, rounded side down, in the center of a serving plate. Cover with the filling mixture, reserving about 1/2 cup. Set the second cake on top and cover with the 1/2 cup filling. Finally, sprinkle the crumb topping over the top.

GOOEY CHOCOLATE CAKE

Cake Ingredients:
1 box gluten free chocolate cake mix
1 cup whole milk
2/3 cup butter, melted
3 eggs
1 cup chopped pecans

Topping Ingredients:
1 1/2 cups granulated sugar
1/2 cup cocoa
1 1/2 cups brown sugar
Ice cream (optional)

Directions:
Preheat oven to 350 degrees. Spray a 9 x 13-inch cake pan with non-stick cooking spray. In a mixing bowl, combine the cake mix, milk, butter, and eggs. Stir in the chopped pecans and then pour batter into the prepared pan. In a bowl, mix together the topping ingredients and sprinkle over the batter. Pour 2 cups of cold water over the batter mixture. Bake for 30 to 35 minutes or until surface of cake looks pretty "set" when you jiggle the pan. When serving, turn pieces upside-down and top with ice cream.

A MIDSUMMER'S DELIGHT CAKE

Cake Ingredients:
1 box gluten free yellow cake mix
1/2 cup sour cream
1 cup water
1/2 cup (1 stick) butter, melted
2 tsp vanilla extract
4 eggs

Topping Ingredients:
1 cup sour cream
1 8-oz container frozen whipped topping, thawed
1 1/2 cups powdered sugar
Seasonal fresh fruit (strawberries, blueberries, raspberries, blackberries), rinsed and patted dry

Directions:
Preheat oven to 325 degrees. Spray a 9 x 13-inch cake pan with non-stick cooking spray and set aside. Using an electric mixer, blend the cake ingredients and pour into the prepared pan. Bake for 25 minutes or until a toothpick inserted in center comes out clean. Remove from the oven and let cool. For the frosting, combine the sour cream, whipped topping, and powdered sugar in a medium-size bowl and blend with an electric mixer until light and fluffy. Spread the frosting mixture over the cake and then arrange the fruit on top.

LUSCIOUS LAYERED TIRAMISU

Ingredients:
1 package gluten free yellow cake mix
3 eggs
1/2 cup butter, melted
1/2 cup milk
1 tsp instant coffee powder
1/2 to 3/4 cup coffee, brewed extra strong

Filling Ingredients:
1 8-oz container mascarpone cheese
1/2 cup powdered sugar
2 Tbsp brewed coffee

Frosting Ingredients:
2 cups heavy cream
1/4 cup powdered sugar
2 Tbsp brewed coffee
1 tsp dark cocoa

Directions:
Preheat oven to 350 degrees. Spray 2 cake pans with non-stick cooking spray. Blend the cake mix, eggs, butter, and milk together with an electric mixer. Pour batter into cake pans and bake for 20 to 25 minutes, or until a toothpick inserted into the center of the cake comes out clean. Let cakes cool in pan, then invert onto a wire rack to cool completely.
For the filling: Using an electric mixer, combine mascarpone, 1/2 cup powdered sugar and 2 Tbsp coffee; beat just until smooth.
For the frosting: Using an electric mixer, beat the cream, 1/4 cup powdered sugar, 2 Tbsp coffee, and dark cocoa until stiff peaks form.
To assemble: Place one cake layer on a serving plate. Using a thin skewer, poke holes in the cake, about 1 inch apart. Pour 1/4 cup brewed coffee over the cake, allowing it to soak in. Spread the filling mixture on top of this first layer. Top with the second cake layer, repeating the steps of poking holes and pouring coffee over the top. Spread the sides and top of cake with frosting. If desired, place cocoa in a sieve and lightly dust top of cake. Refrigerate at least 30 minutes before serving.

A MIDNIGHT BITE CAKE

Ingredients:
2 cups gluten free flour mix
1 cup granulated sugar
2 tsp baking soda
1/2 cup cocoa
1 cup cold water
1 cup mayonnaise
1 tsp vanilla extract
1 1/2 cups mini chocolate chips

Glaze:
1/2 cup powdered sugar
1-2 tsp milk

Directions:
Preheat oven to 350 degrees. Spray a 9 x13 inch baking dish with non-stick cooking spray. Using an electric mixer, combine and blend together all ingredients except the chocolate chips. Stir in the chocolate chips. Pour the batter into the prepared pan and bake for 45 minutes, or until a toothpick inserted comes out clean. Cool on a wire rack.

To make the glaze:
Whisk together powdered sugar and enough milk to make a thin glaze. Drizzle the glaze over the cooled cake.

SOUTHERN BUTTER CAKE WITH A TWIST

Ingredients:
1 package gluten free lemon cake mix
1/2 cup (1 stick) butter, melted
1 egg
1 tsp lemon extract
1 tsp almond extract
1/3 cup poppy seeds
1 8-oz package cream cheese, softened
2 eggs
1 tsp vanilla
1/2 cup (1 stick) butter, melted
2 cups powdered sugar

Directions:
Preheat oven to 350 degrees. Spray a 9 x 13-inch baking pan with non-stick cooking spray. Using an electric mixer, combine the cake mix, butter, egg, extracts, and poppy seeds. Pat the mixture into the bottom of the baking pan. In a large bowl, beat the cream cheese until smooth. Add the eggs, vanilla, and butter, beating well. Add the powdered sugar. Spread over cake batter and bake for 40 to 50 minutes. Do not over bake. The center should to be gooey.

STRAWBERRY RHUBARB CUSTARD CAKE

Ingredients:
1 box gluten free yellow cake mix
2 eggs
2/3 cup butter, melted
1/2 cup milk
2 cups fresh rhubarb, chopped
2 cups fresh strawberries, sliced
1 cup sugar
1 cup whipping cream
Sweetened whipped cream for garnish

Directions:
Preheat oven to 350 degrees. Spray a 9 x 13-inch baking pan with non-stick cooking spray. Using an electric mixer, combine the cake mix, eggs, butter, and milk. Pour into the prepared pan. Spread the rhubarb and strawberries evenly over the batter. Sprinkle the sugar over the fruit and then pour the cream over the batter and fruit. Bake for 40 to 45 minutes or until golden brown. Serve each slice with a dollop of whipped cream on top.

MINI UPSIDE-DOWN PINEAPPLE CAKES

Ingredients:
1 cup butter, divided
1 cup brown sugar
1/4 tsp cinnamon
1 14-oz can sliced pineapple rings, drained with juice reserved
Maraschino cherries
1 vanilla or yellow gluten free boxed cake mix
3 eggs, beaten
3/4 cup whole milk
1 tsp vanilla extract
Sweetened whipped cream

Directions:
Preheat the oven to 325 degrees. Spray 6 single serving size, oven-proof bowls with non-stick cooking spray. In a small saucepan, melt the 1 cup butter. Remove and set aside 1/3 cup of the melted butter to use later. Add the brown sugar, cinnamon and reserved pineapple juice to the 2/3 butter still heating in the saucepan. Stir the mixture frequently, until the brown sugar has dissolved. Divide the brown sugar mixture evenly into the bottom of each bowl and set one pineapple ring on top of each. Place a cherry in the center of each pineapple ring. Using an electric mixer, combine the cake mix, the reserved 1/3 cup melted butter, eggs, milk and vanilla. Divide the batter evenly between the bowls. Bake for 20 to 25 minutes or until a toothpick inserted into the center comes out clean. Remove from oven, and while still warm, slip a knife around the edge of the cake to loosen and then turn upside-down onto individual serving plates. Spoon any excess topping from the bowls back onto the cakes. Serve warm with a dollop of sweetened whipped cream.

SURPRISING RED VELVET CAKE

Ingredients:
1/3 cup gluten free buttermilk
3 eggs
1 tsp vanilla extract
2 cups quinoa, cooked and cooled
1/2 cup (1 stick) butter, melted
1 1/2 cups granulated sugar
3 Tbsp cocoa
4 tsp red food coloring
1 tsp baking powder
1 tsp salt
1 Tbsp white vinegar
1/2 tsp baking soda

Frosting:
2 1/4 cups whipping cream
1 1/4 cups semi-sweet chocolate chips

Directions:
Preheat the oven to 350 degrees. Spray two 8-inch round cake pans with non-stick cooking spray. Using a food processor or blender, combine the buttermilk, eggs and vanilla. Process just until light and fluffy. Add the cooked quinoa and the butter. Blend until smooth. In a large bowl, whisk together the sugar, cocoa, food coloring, baking powder and salt. Add the contents from the blender and mix with a wooden spoon or whisk until combined. Measure the vinegar into a small dish and add the baking soda – it will foam. After a minute, stir to dissolve the soda then gently stir into the cake batter. Divide the batter evenly between the two pans and bake for about 30 minutes or until a knife or toothpick inserted in the center comes out clean.

For the frosting, place the chocolate chips in a medium bowl. Heat the whipping cream in a saucepan until it almost boils. Pour the hot cream over the chocolate chips and let the mixture sit for five minutes. Whisk to combine until it is glossy and smooth. Cover the bowl with plastic wrap and refrigerate 2 to 3 hours. When completely chilled, use an electric mixer to whip the mixture to soft peaks. Spread the frosting over the top of one. Place one cake layer upside down on a serving platter or plate. Cover with frosting then set the second cake layer upside down on top of the frosted layer. Spread the remaining frosting over the top of the cake. If desired, frost the sides of the cake. Chill for at least 2 hours before serving.

STRAWBERRIES AND CREAM CAKE

Ingredients:

2 cups gluten free all-purpose flour mix
1 tsp baking powder
1/2 tsp baking soda
1/2 cup (one stick) butter, softened
1 3/4 cups sugar
4 egg whites, at room temperature
1 tsp vanilla
2/3 cup milk
2/3 cup sour cream
2 cups sliced fresh strawberries, sprinkled with sugar, or frozen strawberries in syrup, thawed
1 pint heavy cream, chilled
1/4 cup powdered sugar
1 tsp vanilla extract

Directions:

Preheat oven to 350 degrees. Spray three 9-inch round cake pans with non-stick cooking spray. In a medium bowl, whisk together flour, baking powder, and baking soda in medium bowl and set aside. Using an electric mixer, cream together butter and sugar. Add egg whites and vanilla and beat for about 30 seconds. Reduce speed to low, and add flour mixture, milk, and sour cream. Beat about a minute longer then pour into prepared pans. Bake for 18 to 22 minutes, or until lightly golden and toothpick comes out clean. Cool in pans on racks, then remove cakes from pans and cool completely. Beat the cream, powdered sugar, and vanilla on high speed until soft peaks form.

Place one of the cake layers on a plate, and spread with 1/2 cup of the sweetened whipped cream. Spoon half of the sliced strawberries evenly on top. Spread another 1/2 cup whipped cream on top of the strawberries. Place the second cake layer on top of the first and repeat the layers of whipped cream and strawberries. Top with the final cake layer, and cover completely with the remaining whipped cream. Garnish with strawberries, as desired. Refrigerate.

FRESH PEACH SKILLET CAKE

Ingredients:
1/3 cup butter
1 cup sugar, divided
1 tsp cinnamon
1/2 tsp almond extract
5-6 fresh peaches, sliced and peeled,
or 2 29-oz cans, drained
1/2 cup sliced almonds, toasted
1 cup gluten free flour mix
1/4 tsp cinnamon
3 Tbsp butter, melted
1 egg, well beaten
1/3 cup evaporated milk
1/3 cup water

Directions:
Melt butter in a large skillet. Stir in 2/3 cup sugar, 1 tsp cinnamon, and almond extract. Add peach slices to the skillet; cover and cook over medium heat for 5 minutes. Top with toasted almonds. In a separate bowl, stir together flour, 1/3 cup sugar, and 1/4 tsp cinnamon. Combine 3 Tbsp melted butter, egg, milk, and water in separate bowl. Add liquid to flour mixture, blending until just moistened. Spoon over hot peaches and almonds. Cover tightly and cook on the stove-top on very low heat for 20 to 25 minutes or until set. Invert onto a serving plate.

VANILLA CAKE WITH PRALINE TOPPING

Ingredients:
2 Tbsp butter
1 1/2 cups gluten free flour mixture
3/4 tsp baking powder
1/4 tsp baking soda
3/4 tsp salt
1 cup sugar
6 Tbsp butter, softened
2 eggs
1 Tbsp vanilla
3/4 cup buttermilk

For the Praline Sauce:
3/4 cup brown sugar
1/2 cup butter
1/4 cup cream
1/8 tsp salt
1 tsp vanilla extract
1 cup coarsely chopped pecans or walnuts
Vanilla ice cream (optional)

Directions:
In a large skillet, melt the 2 Tbsp butter. In a medium bowl, sift together the flour mixture, baking powder, baking soda and salt. Set aside. In another bowl, using an electric mixer, cream the sugar and butter, until light and fluffy. Add the eggs, beating well to incorporate. Add the vanilla and buttermilk. With the mixer on low, add the dry ingredients. Beat until well combined, stirring by hand if necessary. Pour the batter into the skillet. Cook the cake, covered tightly, on very low heat for 30 to 35 minutes. Meanwhile, make the praline sauce. Combine the brown sugar, butter, cream and salt in a medium skillet or saucepan. Bring to a boil, stirring for 3 minutes. Remove from heat and stir in the vanilla and nuts. Allow to set for 15 minutes then pour over the top of the cooked skillet cake. Serve warm with vanilla ice cream.

HAWAIIAN ISLAND DUMP CAKE

Ingredients:
2 21-oz cans pineapple chunks (including liquid)
1 6-oz jar maraschino cherries (drained)
1/2 cup sweetened flake coconut
1/2 cup macadamia nuts, chopped
1/2 cup brown sugar, packed
1 box gluten free yellow or white cake mix
1 cup (2 sticks) butter

Directions:
Preheat oven to 350 degrees. Spray a 9 x 13-inch baking dish with non-stick spray. Pour pineapple (including liquid) into the bottom of baking dish and then add the cherries, distributing evenly. Sprinkle the coconut, macadamia nuts and brown sugar over the cherries. Spread the cake mix on top of all. Slice butter into pats and place evenly on the cake mix, covering the entire top. Bake for 45 to 60 minutes or until the top is golden brown and cake is bubbly.

PICNIC CAKE

Ingredients:
2 eggs
1 cup brown sugar
1/2 tsp salt
1 large ripe banana, mashed (about 1/2 cup)
1/2 cup canola oil
1 1/2 tsp vanilla extract
1 14.5 oz can crushed pineapple (with syrup)
1 1/4 cup gluten free flour mixture
1/2 tsp baking soda
1/2 tsp cinnamon
2/3 cup pecans, chopped (plus garnish)
1 16-oz container prepared cream cheese frosting

Directions:
Preheat oven to 350 degrees. Spray an 8 x 8-inch baking dish with non-stick cooking spray. To the prepared dish, add the eggs, brown sugar, salt, banana, oil, and vanilla, whisking until completely combined. Stir in the pineapple (with liquid). Add the flour, baking soda, cinnamon, and chopped pecans to the bowl, and whisk until combined. Bake until top is set and toothpick inserted into the center comes out clean, 35 to 40 minutes. Cool completely. If desired, spread prepared cream cheese frosting over the top, and sprinkle with additional pecans.

SWEET LEMON SLOW COOKER CAKE

Ingredients:
1 box gluten free yellow cake mix
1/2 cup fresh or prepared lemon juice (if juicing fresh lemons, this could be done in advance and refrigerated)
1/2 cup water
1/3 cup butter, melted
3 eggs, well beaten
1 Tbsp lemon zest
1/2 cup white chocolate chips
Vanilla ice cream (optional)

Directions:
Spray slow cooker with non-stick cooking spray. Add the cake mix, lemon juice, water, melted butter, eggs, and lemon zest, and whisk together with a fork. Batter will have some lumps. Spread the batter evenly on the bottom of the slow cooker. Sprinkle the white chocolate chips on top. Cook on high for 1 1/2 to 2 hours. The cake will be very moist. Scoop into bowls, and serve warm with vanilla ice cream.

GLUTEN FREE GRAHAM CRACKER PIE CRUST

Ingredients:
1 Tbsp powdered sugar
1 3/4 cups crushed gluten free graham crackers
(or other gluten free cookies)
8 Tbsp (1 stick) butter, melted

Directions:
Spray the bottom and sides of a pie plate with non-stick cooking spray. In a medium bowl, combine the powdered sugar and crushed cracker crumbs. Add the butter, stirring until the mixture sticks together. Using the back of a spoon, press the mixture into the bottom and sides of the pie plate. Pour your favorite gluten-free pie filling into the crust and bake.

GRANDMA'S CLASSIC CRUST (BUT GLUTEN FREE)

Ingredients:
1/4 cup brown rice flour
1/2 cup sweet rice flour
1/4 cup of cornstarch
1/2 tsp guar gum
1/4 tsp salt
6 Tbsp unsalted butter
1 egg

Directions:
In a medium bowl, combine the flours, cornstarch, guar gum, and salt. Cut in butter with a pastry blender or two knives until the mixture resembles coarse crumbs. If preferred, a food processer works well for this step. Add the egg, and just enough water to form a ball that will stay together. Roll the dough out with a rolling pin on a rice-floured surface or waxed paper until it reaches the size needed for your pie plate. Carefully peel back the dough and turn into the pie plate. Cut off excess, crimp edges and fill with your favorite filling.

NO-BAKE PEACHES AND CREAM CHEESE PIE

Ingredients:
1 gluten free graham cracker or vanilla wafer pie crust
1 8-oz package of cream cheese, softened
1/4 cup sugar
1/8 tsp almond extract
1 Tbsp orange juice
1 1/2 cups frozen creamy whipped dessert topping, thawed
3 cups fresh peaches, peeled and sliced
1/4 cup honey roasted sliced almonds

Directions:
Using an electric mixer, combine the cream cheese, sugar, almond extract, and orange juice until smooth. Gently stir whipped topping into the cream cheese mixture and pour into the crust. Cover and refrigerate for an hour or more. Before serving, arrange peach slices over the filling and sprinkle the honey roasted almonds on top.

FRENCH COUNTRY COCONUT PIE

Ingredients:
3 eggs, beaten
1 1/2 cups sugar
1/2 cup (1 stick) butter, melted
1 Tbsp white vinegar
1 tsp vanilla extract
Dash of salt
1 cup sweetened flaked coconut
1 whole 9" uncooked gluten free pie shell

Directions:
Preheat oven to 350 degrees. Using an electric mixer, combine all ingredients except the coconut. Stir in the coconut and pour into the pie shell. Bake for 1 hour or until golden brown on top.

CHOCOLATE PEPPERMINT PIE

Ingredients:
3/4 cup (1 1/2 sticks) butter
1 cup sugar
2 oz unsweetened chocolate
1/2 tsp vanilla extract
3 eggs
1 gluten-free chocolate cookie pie crust
1 pint heavy whipping cream
1/3 cup sugar
1/2 tsp peppermint extract
1/4 cup hard peppermint candies, crushed

Directions:
In the bowl of an electric mixer, whip butter and sugar. Melt chocolate on the stove or in microwave, stirring. Add vanilla. Add the chocolate to sugar mixture. Add eggs, 1 at a time, beating well between each addition. Pour into crust and refrigerate. Beat whipping cream, adding sugar and peppermint extract, until soft peaks form. Stir in the crushed candy pieces (reserve a bit for the top). Spread the whipped cream over the chocolate. Garnish with the reserved candy pieces.

EASY LEMON PIE

Ingredients:
1 prepared gluten free graham cracker crust
2 (14-oz) cans sweetened condensed milk
1/3 cup lemon juice
1 tsp grated lemon peel
1 spray can sweetened whipped cream
Sugared lemon peel spirals

Directions:
Preheat oven to 350 degrees. Bake prepared crust for 10-15 minutes until slightly browned. Whisk together the sweetened condensed milk, lemon juice, and grated lemon peel. Pour into the crust. Refrigerate for 3 to 4 hours. Just before serving, spray the whipped cream around the edge and in the middle of the pie for decoration. Garnish with sugared lemon peel spirals.

PUMPKIN STREUSEL PIE WITH SPICED CREAM

Ingredients:
1 gluten free pie crust
1/2 cup brown sugar
1/4 cup gluten free flour mix
1/2 cup chopped pecans
4 Tbsp (1/2 stick) butter
1 3/4 cups pumpkin
2 eggs
1 cup sugar
1 tsp vanilla
1 1/4 tsp cinnamon
1/2 tsp nutmeg
1/2 tsp ginger
1/4 tsp salt
1 10.5-oz can evaporated milk

Topping Ingredients:
1 cup whipping cream
1/4 cup sugar
1/4 tsp cinnamon (more or less as desired)
1/4 tsp nutmeg (more or less as desired)

Directions:
Preheat oven to 400 degrees. Bake prepared crust for 10 minutes then remove. In a smaller bowl, combine the brown sugar, flour, and pecans. Cut the butter in until mixture resembles coarse crumbs to make streusel topping. Set aside. Using an electric mixer, mix pumpkin and eggs; add sugar, vanilla and spices. Mix in milk. Pour into pie crust. Sprinkle the streusel on top and bake for 15 minutes. Lower heat to 350 and continue baking 35 to 45 minutes or until toothpick inserted in center comes out clean. Whip cream until soft peaks have formed, adding the sugar and spices to taste. Serve each piece of pie with a dollop of spiced whipped cream.

SUMMERY STRAWBERRY PIE

Ingredients:
1 gluten free pie crust
2 8-oz packages of cream cheese, softened
1 cup sugar, divided 3/4 and 1/4 cups
1/2 tsp vanilla extract
2 eggs
1 8-oz container sour cream
2-3 pints fresh strawberries, washed and hulled

Directions:
Preheat oven to 400 degrees. Bake the pie crust for 5-7 minutes, remove pie crust and turn heat down to warm. Using an electric mixer, combine cream cheese, 3/4 cups sugar, and vanilla. Add eggs and mix well. Pour mixture into pie crust. In a small bowl, combine the sour cream and 1/4 cup sugar. Spread sour cream mixture over cream cheese mixture in pie crust. Put in warm oven for 10 to 15 minutes. Remove from oven to refrigerator for 2-4 hours. Before serving, set the strawberries one at a time with their tops facing down until the top of the pie is covered.

TOFFEE APPLE ICE-CREAM PIE

Ingredients:
1 egg
3/4 cup sugar
1 tsp baking powder
1/4 cup gluten free flour mix
1/2 cup tart apples, peeled, pared, chopped fine
1/2 cup walnuts, chopped
1 1/2 quarts vanilla bean ice cream, softened
3 gluten free chocolate covered toffee candy bars

Directions:
Preheat oven to 350 degrees. Spray a 10-inch pie plate with non-stick cooking spray. In a mixing bowl, combine egg, sugar, baking powder, and flour mix. Beat well. Stir in the apples and nuts. Pour into the prepared dish, pushing up the sides of the dish. Bake for 25 minutes. Crust will rise and then fall during cooking. Remove from oven and cool. Soften ice cream slightly and spoon into the shell. Crush toffee bars and sprinkle over ice cream. Cover with foil and store in the freezer until ready to serve. Remove from freezer 15 minutes before serving.

NUTTY PINEAPPLE CREAM PIE

Ingredients:
24 gluten free vanilla wafers, crushed and divided
1/2 cup (1 stick) butter, softened
2 cups powdered sugar
2 eggs
1 cup walnuts or pecans, chopped
1 tsp vanilla
1 cup whipped cream, whipped
1 cup crushed pineapple, drained

Directions:
Put crushed vanilla wafers into bottom of a pie plate, reserving 1/4 cup for topping. Using an electric mixer, cream butter and sugar. Add eggs, nuts and vanilla, beating well. Pour over the vanilla wafers. In a medium bowl, combine whipped cream and pineapple. Pour over first layer and then top with remaining crushed wafers. Refrigerate overnight.

EASIEST EVER BANANA CREAM PIE

Ingredients:
1 gluten free pie crust
3 to 4 bananas, peeled and sliced (save one for top)
1 3/4 cup milk
1 3.4 oz box gluten free banana cream pudding mix
1 8-oz container frozen whipped topping, divided

Directions:
Preheat oven to 400 degrees. Bake crust for 10 to 15 minutes until slightly browned. Cool. Slice 3 bananas to form a layer in the bottom of the crust. In a medium bowl, whisk together the milk and pudding mix. Fold in 2/3 of the frozen topping. Pour into the pie crust and refrigerate. Just before serving, spread remaining whipped topping over the pudding. Slice last banana and place evenly on top of pie.

COCONUT CREAM PIE

Ingredients:
2 cups whole milk or half and half
2 cups sweetened shredded coconut
1 tsp vanilla
2 eggs
1 cup sugar, divided (3/4 cup and 1/4 cup)
1 cup large-shred coconut pieces
1/4 cup gluten free flour mix
1 gluten free graham cracker or shortbread cookie crust
1 1/2 cups whipping cream

Directions:
Preheat oven to 350 degrees. In a large saucepan, combine the milk and 2 cups shredded coconut. Cook, stirring, until mixture is nearly boiling. Remove from heat. In a small bowl, whisk together the vanilla, eggs, 3/4 cups of sugar, and the flour. When blended completely, slowly pour in the milk, whisking to combine, then pour back into the saucepan and cook over medium heat, stirring until mixture thickens and starts to bubble. Cover and cool with a piece of plastic wrap on the surface to prevent a "skin" from forming. Spread large-shred coconut on a baking sheet and bake for 5 to 7 minutes or until golden brown – watch carefully to prevent over cooking. When pie filling is completely cool, pour into the crust. Beat whipping cream and reserved 1/4 cup sugar together until soft peaks form. Spoon whipped cream onto top of pie. Garnish the top of the pie with the toasted coconut.

ROCKY MOUNTAIN MUD PIE

Ingredients:
20 gluten free chocolate sandwich cookies, crushed
1/4-1/2 cup (1/2-1 stick) butter, melted
1.5-quart carton coffee flavored ice cream, softened
Chocolate covered toffee candy bars, chopped (gluten free)
1 jar hot fudge sauce (gluten free)

Directions:
Put the crushed cookies in the bottom of a pie plate. Drizzle the melted butter over the cookies and mix it in with a fork—add just enough melted butter so the cookies stick together. Press the cookies into the sides and bottom of the pie plate to make the crust. Spoon the softened ice cream into the cookie crust, smoothing out the top with a spatula or knife if needed. Sprinkle the chopped candy pieces on top. Freeze until firm, six hours or overnight. Serve with hot fudge spooned over the top of each piece.

ELEGANT PEARS AND CHERRY-CREAM DESSERT

Ingredients:
1 refrigerated or frozen (thawed) gluten free pie crust, rolled out and cut into 4 squares
4 Tbsp (1/2 stick) butter, divided
2 Tbsp granulated sugar
1 egg, beaten
3/4 cup mascarpone cheese
1/4 cup powdered sugar
1/2 cup heavy cream
1/2 tsp vanilla
Dash of ground nutmeg
2 large pears, peeled and halved
Sprinkling of sugar
1 cup fresh sweet cherries, pitted
Balsamic Fig Glaze (finishing drizzle, optional))

Directions:
In a large skillet, melt half of the butter. Place the dough squares into the skillet and cook until golden and crispy, turning over halfway through cooking. Remove to paper towel to cool. Sprinkle with sugar and set aside. In a bowl, combine the egg, mascarpone, powdered sugar, cream, vanilla, and nutmeg, blending until creamy and smooth. Refrigerate. Return the skillet to medium heat, melt the remaining 2 Tbsp butter. Put the pear halves in, sprinkle with sugar and cook about 2 minutes on each side. Turn off heat. To assemble the dessert, place in order on each plate, one pie crust wedge, a pear half, a scant drizzle of balsamic glaze (or to your taste), a dollop of the mascarpone mixture, and 3 cherries set on top of the mascarpone.

QUICK KEY LIME CHEESECAKE

Ingredients:
1 14-oz can sweetened condensed milk
1 8-oz package of cream cheese, softened
1 8-oz tub of frozen whipped topping, thawed
1/3 cup of fresh lime juice
1 prepared gluten free crust
1 16-oz container sour cream
3 Tbsp sugar
Thin lime slices

Directions:
Using an electric mixer, combine all ingredients, except the lime juice. Blend until light and fluffy. Add lime juice and blend well. Pour mixture into the pie crust. Stir together the sour cream and sugar. Spread over the top of the cheesecake and garnish with lime slices.

CHOCOLATE PECAN PIE SQUARES

Ingredients:
3 1/2 cups gluten free all-purpose flour mix
1 1/2 cups powdered sugar
1/2 cup unsweetened cocoa powder
1/2 tsp salt
1 1/2 cups (3 sticks) butter, cubed
2 cups semi-sweet chocolate chips
1 cup brown sugar, firmly packed
1 cup light corn syrup
1/2 cup (1 stick) butter, melted
3 eggs, lightly beaten
1 Tbsp vanilla extract
3 1/2 cups pecans, toasted and roughly chopped (save some whole pecans for top crust)
Vanilla ice cream (optional)

Directions:
Preheat oven to 350 degrees. Spray a 9 x 13-inch pan with non-stick cooking spray. In the bottom of the prepared pan, whisk together flour, sugar, cocoa powder and salt. Add butter and crumble into the mixture with your fingers. Remove 1 cup of the crust mixture and set aside for topping. Press remaining crust into the bottom of the pan. Sprinkle with chocolate chips. In a large bowl, whisk together the brown sugar, corn syrup, butter, eggs and vanilla. Stir in the chopped pecans and pour this mixture over the crust. Spread reserved crust over the pecan mixture. Top with whole pecans. Bake 40 to 45 minutes or until golden. Cool completely on a wire rack.
Delicious with vanilla ice cream.

AFTERNOON MACAROONS

Ingredients:
4 large egg whites
1/2 cup sugar
1 tsp vanilla
1/4 tsp salt
3 cups sweetened, shredded coconut (if desired, can be toasted)
1/2 cup semi-sweet chocolate chips, melted

Directions:
Preheat the oven to 350 degrees. Spray an 8 x 8-inch baking dish with non-stick cooking spray. Combine the egg whites, sugar, vanilla, and salt in the dish. Whisk until the whites and sugar are completely combined and the mixture is frothy. Add the coconut to the egg mixture and stir until the coconut is evenly moistened. Press firmly in the bottom of the dish. Bake the macaroon bars for 15 to 20 minutes, until golden. Let cool for 5 minutes, then flip upside down onto a plate or cutting board. Drizzle with melted chocolate before cutting into squares.

Cookies and Bars

FILLED SHORTBREAD COOKIES

Ingredients:
2 cups almond flour
1/4 cup coconut flour, sifted if lumpy
1/2 cup granulated sugar
1 tsp baking powder
1/8 tsp salt
7 Tbsp refined coconut oil, melted and slightly cooled
1 egg, room temperature
1 tsp almond extract
1/2 cup apricot or peach jam (or jam of choice)

Directions:
Preheat the oven to 350 degrees. Spray a cookie sheet with non-stick cooking spray. In a medium bowl, stir together the almond flour, coconut flour, sugar, baking powder and salt. In another medium bowl, stir together the coconut oil, egg and almond extract. Add the dry ingredients to the liquid ingredients and stir until combined. Let sit for 10 minutes. Roll the dough into tablespoon size balls and place on cookie sheet. Using a teaspoon, make an impression on the top of each dough ball and spoon a bit of jam into that spot. Bake for 7 to 8 minutes or until the cookies have barely started browning around the edges. Let the cookies set on the baking sheet for a few minutes before removing them to a wire rack.

SUMPTUOUS PUMPKIN OATMEAL COOKIES

Ingredients:
1 Tbsp ground flaxseed meal
1 Tbsp water
1/2 cup (1 stick) butter, softened
3/4 cup brown sugar, packed
1 egg
1 tsp vanilla
1 tsp baking soda
1 tsp cinnamon
1/4 tsp salt
3/4 cup canned pumpkin
1 1/4 cups gluten free oat flour
1 cup rice flour (or gluten free flour mix)
1 1/4 cup gluten free rolled oats
1 cup chocolate chips

Directions:
Preheat oven to 350 degrees. Spray a cookie sheet with non-stick cooking spray. Dissolve flaxseed meal in the water. Set aside. Combine butter, brown sugar, egg, vanilla, baking soda, cinnamon, salt, and pumpkin. Stir until smooth. Add flours, oats, and chocolate chips and stir until well-blended. Drop by spoonfuls onto cookie sheet. Bake for 15 to 17 minutes.

Cookies and Bars

LIKE MAGIC BARS
BECAUSE THEY DISAPPEAR FAST—LIKE MAGIC!

Ingredients:
1 3/4 cups gluten free gingersnap cookies, crushed
1/4 cup packed brown sugar
4 Tbsp (1/2 stick) unsalted butter, melted
2 cups shredded coconut
2/3 cups sliced almonds
1 14-oz bag semi-sweet mini chocolate chips
1 14-oz can sweetened condensed milk

Directions:
Preheat oven to 350 degrees. In a large bowl, whisk together gingersnap crumbs, brown sugar and butter and stir until mixture is well combined and the crumbs hold together. If needed, add a bit more butter. Press crumb mixture into an 8 x 8-inch baking dish, evenly covering the bottom and sides. In a large bowl, mix coconut, almonds, chocolate chips, and sweetened condensed milk. Spread on top of gingersnap crust. Bake for 12 to 15 min or until golden brown.

BLACK FOREST BROWNIES

Ingredients:
1 15-oz can dark sweet cherries (drained, reserve syrup)
2 Tbsp cornstarch
1 cup gluten free flour
1 cup sugar
1/2 cup cocoa powder
1/2 cup (1 stick) butter, softened
1 egg
1 cup semi-sweet chocolate chips
Cherry vanilla ice cream (optional)

Directions:
In a skillet, combine cornstarch and the reserved cherry syrup. Heat and stir until thickened, stir in cherries, remove to a bowl and set aside to cool. In a large bowl, stir together the flour, sugar, cocoa powder, butter and egg until crumbly. Set aside 1 1/2 cups of crumb mixture. Press the remaining brownie mixture into the skillet. Spread cooled cherry mixture over top of brownies in the skillet. Sprinkle with chocolate chips. Sprinkle reserved crumb mixture over top. Cook in the skillet on low heat, covered, for 20 to 25 minutes, carefully lifting up the edges every few minutes to make sure it is not burning on the bottom. Cut into wedges and serve warm with cherry-vanilla ice cream.

Cookies and Bars

CAMPING COOKIES

Ingredients:

2 1/4 cups gluten free all-purpose flour mix
1/2 tsp baking soda
1 cup (2 sticks) butter, softened
1 cup brown sugar
1/2 cup sugar
1 tsp salt
2 tsp vanilla extract
2 eggs
2 cups white chocolate chips
1/2 cup pecans, chopped
1/2 cup gluten free oatmeal
1/2 cup gluten-free toffee candy pieces
2 tsp butter

Directions:

In a small bowl, whisk together the flour and baking soda; set aside. Using an electric mixer, combine the butter and sugars; beat on medium speed until light and fluffy. Reduce speed to low; add the salt, vanilla, and eggs. Beat until well mixed, about 1 minute. Add flour mixture; mix until just combined. Stir in the white chocolate chips, pecans, oatmeal, and toffee pieces. Put about 2 tsp butter in a non-stick skillet, melting over medium heat until it covers the bottom of the pan. Spoon dough by tablespoon into the skillet, leaving room between cookies. Press down tops with the bottom of a drinking glass. Cover the pan with a lid and bake for about 5 minutes. Be careful to keep the heat low so the cookies don't burn. Lift the cover and flip the cookies with a spatula. Bake again for another 5 minutes with the pan covered. Remove the cookies to a wire rack to cool.

CHUNKY CHOCOLATE COCONUT COOKIES

Ingredients:
1 14-oz bag semi-sweet chocolate chips
1 13.5-oz can full-fat coconut milk
2 cups sweetened shredded coconut
1/2 cup pecans, chopped
1/3 cup honey

Directions:
Preheat oven to 350 degrees. Spray a cookie sheet with non-stick cooking spray. Mix all ingredients in a bowl until well combined. Drop dough by tablespoon onto cookie sheet. Bake for 12 to 15 min or until golden brown.

HAPPY HIKER BARS

Ingredients:
1/2 cup almond butter
3/4 cup coconut
1/2 cup honey-roasted sunflower kernels
1/2 cup gluten free quick oats
1/4 cup ground flaxseed meal
1/4 cup honey
1/2 tsp almond extract
1/2 cup mini chocolate chips

Directions:
Place all ingredients except chocolate chips into an 8 x 8-inch pan. Stir to blend. Press down into bottom of pan. Sprinkle chocolate chips on top and press down again. Cover and refrigerate. When ready to serve, cut into squares.

LEMON SPARKLE BARS

Ingredients:
1 gluten free angel food cake mix
1 22-oz can lemon pie filling
1/4 cup decorator's sugar (large crystal)

Directions:
Preheat oven to 350 degrees. Spray a 9 x 13-inch pan with non-stick cooking spray. In a medium bowl, stir together the cake mix and the pie filling. Sprinkle the top with decorator's sugar. Bake for about 35 minutes until cooked through. Let cool before cutting into bars or squares.

Cookies and Bars

SUGARED GINGER COOKIES

Ingredients:
1/2 cup refined coconut oil, melted and slightly cooled
1/2 cup granulated sugar, plus more for rolling the cookies
1/2 cup molasses
1 egg
2 cups gluten free flour blend
1 1/2 tsp cinnamon
1 tsp ground ginger
1/2 tsp baking soda
1/8 tsp salt
1 tsp baking powder

Directions:
Preheat oven to 325 degrees. Spray a cookie sheet with non-stick cooking spray. With an electric mixer, blend coconut oil, sugar, and molasses. Beat until creamy. Add egg, continuing to beat together. Blend in dry ingredients with mixer, changing the attachment when the dough becomes stiff. Using your hands, shape the dough into a ball, cover and chill. When dough has chilled, roll out on a gluten free floured board to 1/8" thick and cut into shapes with cookie cutters. Sprinkle with sugar. Alternatively, roll dough into 1" balls and then roll in sugar. Place the balls of dough on the cookie sheet and flatten with the bottom of a drinking glass. Bake 7 to 9 minutes.

SUGAR BEARS

Ingredients:
3 1/2 cups gluten free flour mix
1 cup granulated sugar plus more for rolling the dough balls
1 cup powdered sugar
1 1/2 tsp xanthan gum (if not already in the flour mix)
1 1/2 tsp baking powder
3/4 tsp salt
10 Tbsp (1 1/4 stick) butter
10 Tbsp (3/4 cup) shortening
2 eggs
1 Tbsp vanilla extract
Candy coated chocolate candy pieces (gluten-free)

Directions:
Preheat oven to 325 degrees. Spray cookie sheets with non-stick cooking spray. In a mixing bowl, combine the flour, granulated sugar, powdered sugar, xanthan gum, baking powder, and salt. Add the butter, shortening, eggs, and vanilla, mixing well until dough takes shape. Next, form the bear's head by rolling dough into 2-inch balls. Roll each ball in granulated sugar and set on the cookie sheet. Press the dough balls flat with the bottom of a drinking glass. Make the ears by forming two small balls with dough, pressing between fingers to flatten. Set them on the "head" so they resemble a bear's ears. Using the candy pieces, make the face—two eyes and a nose/mouth. Bake until the cookies are slightly browned around the edges about 11 to 12 minutes.

RASPBERRY CREAM CHEESE BARS

Ingredients:
1 box gluten free yellow cake mix
1 cup (2 sticks) butter, melted
1 egg, beaten
4 cups powdered sugar
1 8-oz package of cream cheese, softened
2 eggs, beaten
1/4 cup raspberry preserves or jam
1 tsp vanilla

Directions:
Preheat oven to 350 degrees. Spray a 9 x 13-inch baking dish with non-stick cooking spray. Add the cake mix, butter, and 1 egg to the prepared dish and whisk together with a fork. Press mixture into the bottom of the dish. In a large bowl, mix remaining ingredients together with an electric mixer until smooth. Spread the cream cheese mixture evenly over the cake mixture. Bake for 35 to 40 minutes, until bars are set. Cool before serving.

FAVORITE SNACK BARS

Ingredients:
1 cup extra crunchy peanut butter
1/2 cup packed dark brown sugar
1 large egg
1 cup semi-sweet chocolate chips

Directions:
Preheat oven to 350 degrees. Mix peanut butter, brown sugar, and egg until well blended. Press evenly in bottom of an ungreased 9-inch square baking pan. Bake 20 minutes or until lightly browned. Remove from oven, sprinkle with chips, cover pan loosely with foil. Bake 5 minutes longer to melt chips. Spread chocolate evenly over bottom layer. Cool on wire rack. Chill to set. Cut into bars or squares as desired.

NO BAKE FUDGE COOKIES

Ingredients:
2 cups sugar
1/2 cup (1 stick) butter
1/2 cup milk
1/3 cup unsweetened cocoa powder
2 cups rolled oats
1/2 cup peanut butter
Maraschino or candied cherries, halved

Directions:
Combine sugar, butter, milk, and cocoa in medium saucepan. Bring to a boil and boil one minute. Remove from heat. Stir in oats and peanut butter until well combined. Drop by teaspoons onto wax paper. Press cherry half into each cookie. Let stand until set.

CHOCOLATE KISS KRISPIES

Ingredients:
40 large marshmallows
1/4 cup (1/2 stick) butter
5 to 6 cups gluten-free cocoa-flavored crispy rice cereal
1 cup semi-sweet chocolate chips
12-15 chocolate kisses

Directions:
Spray a 13 x 9-inch baking pan with non-stick cooking spray. In a large, microwave-safe bowl combine the marshmallows and butter. Cook on high in microwave, stirring after each minute. Cook until completely melted and stirred together. Remove from microwave and stir in the cereal until completely coated. Stir in chips reserving some for decorating. Butter your hands and then press mixture evenly in pan. Press a chocolate kiss into the top of the cereal bars every 3 inches or so. Cool. Cut into squares as desired.

BANANA SURPRISE

Ingredients:
4 medium-size ripe bananas
1/2 cup (1 stick) butter, melted
1/2 cup brown sugar
1/4 cup chopped pecans (optional)
Dash of ground cinnamon
Vanilla ice cream
Caramel sauce

Directions:
Preheat the oven to 400 degrees. Leaving the bananas in their peels, cut the end of the tops off. Carefully pull back one section of peel (don't pull it all the way off) to expose the banana. While still in their peels, slice bananas lengthwise. Lay the bananas in an 8 x 8-inch baking dish. Add a spoonful of brown sugar to each banana, tucking the sugar into the sliced space. Next, add a sprinkle of chopped pecans to each banana. Pour the melted butter along the length of the bananas, then sprinkle with cinnamon. Replace the pulled back peeling sections and place the dish in the oven. Heat 5 minutes or until bananas are hot and brown sugar is bubbling. Peels will turn black. Serve in bowls with ice cream and caramel sauce.

FRIED FRUIT COMPOTE

Ingredients:
1 Tbsp butter
1 Tbsp canola oil
Your choice fresh fruit (strawberries, bananas, peaches, grapes, apples), sliced
1 Tbsp honey
1 Tbsp water
1 Tbsp white corn syrup
Cinnamon
Vanilla ice cream (optional)

Directions:
Heat butter and oil in a skillet over medium. Arrange fruit slices in the skillet. Cook for 1 to 2 minutes on each side, until starting to brown. Remove from heat. In a small bowl, whisk together honey, water, corn syrup and cinnamon. Pour over the fruit. Allow to cool and serve in bowls or serve warm over vanilla ice cream.

CHOCOLATE-ALMOND PRETZEL DESSERT

Ingredients:
2 cups semi-sweet chocolate chips
1/4 cup whipping cream
1 1/2 cups powdered sugar
1 cup almond butter
6 Tbsp (3/4 stick) butter, melted
2 1/2 cups gluten-free pretzels, coarsely crushed, divided
1/2 cup honey roasted almonds, chopped

Directions:
Line a 13 x 9-inch pan with foil. Lightly coat the foil with cooking spray; set aside. In a medium skillet, combine chocolate chips, and whipping cream. Stir over low heat until pieces are just melted. In a large mixing bowl, stir together powdered sugar, almond butter, and melted butter. Stir in 2 cups of the crushed pretzels. Press mixture firmly into the bottom of prepared pan. Carefully spoon and spread the chocolate mixture over the crumb mixture in pan. Sprinkle the remaining 1/2 cup crushed pretzels and the almonds evenly over chocolate mixture; press gently. Cover and chill for at least 2 hours. Store in refrigerator.

MIMI'S BERRY DUMPLINGS

Ingredients:
4 cups frozen berry mix
1 Tbsp fresh lemon juice
6 Tbsp sugar, divided
1/4 cup water
1 cup gluten free flour
1 tsp baking powder
1/2 tsp baking soda
1/8 tsp salt
2 Tbsp butter, melted
1/2 cup low-fat buttermilk
1/4 tsp ground cinnamon
1 tsp sugar
Whip cream or vanilla ice cream (optional)

Directions:
In a medium skillet, cook berries, lemon juice, 4 Tbsp sugar, and 1/4 cup water over medium heat until slightly thickened, 11 to 13 minutes. Meanwhile, in a bowl, whisk together flour, baking powder, baking soda, salt, and remaining 2 Tbsp sugar; add melted butter and buttermilk, and stir until a moist dough forms. Divide and spoon 6 dollops of dough over fruit in the skillet. Combine the cinnamon and 1 tsp sugar, and sprinkle over the dough. Cover pan tightly with foil, and cook over medium-low until dumplings are set and tops are dry to the touch, about 15 minutes. Serve warm with whip cream or vanilla ice cream.

CRUNCHY CANDY BITES

Ingredients:
1/2 cup sweetened shredded coconut
1/2 cup pecans, coarsely chopped
1 cup (or more if desired) puffed rice cereal
16-oz gluten free white chocolate candy bark
8-oz.(1/2 of 16-oz container) gluten free salted caramel frosting, warmed

Directions:
Cover a large cookie sheet with a piece of wax paper. Spread the coconut, pecans, and cereal evenly on the cookie sheet. In a microwave-safe bowl, melt the white chocolate bark, stirring in the warmed caramel frosting until the two are just barely blended (stripes of the two are visible). Drizzle the melted bark and frosting over the ingredients on the cookie sheet, using a spatula to stir and coat. Immediately place in the refrigerator to chill. When completely cooled, break into small pieces.

SIMPLY DELICIOUS LAYERED DESSERT DIP

Ingredients:
8-oz cream cheese, softened
1 8-oz container frozen whipped topping, thawed
1/2 cup powdered sugar
1/2 cup mini chocolate chips
Caramel ice cream topping
1 cup toasted coconut
Chocolate ice cream topping
1/2 cup pecans, chopped
Gluten free shortbread cookies
(or other favorite gluten free cookies)

Directions:
In a mixing/serving bowl, combine the cream cheese, frozen whipped topping, and powdered sugar. Stir until well-blended then spoon onto a plate and smooth out the top. Spread the mini chocolate chips over the cream cheese mixture. Drizzle a layer of caramel sauce onto the chocolate chips, and then spread on a layer of toasted coconut. Drizzle on a layer of chocolate sauce and then sprinkle on the pecans. To serve, spoon the dip onto dessert plates and serve with shortbread cookies for dipping.

GLUTEN FREE CAKE DOUGHNUTS

Ingredients:
1 egg
3/4 cup sugar
1/2 cup milk
1/2 tsp salt
1 tsp vanilla
2 tsp baking powder
1 Tbsp butter, melted
3 cups gluten free flour mix
1 tsp xanthan gum (if not already added to flour mix)
2 cups powdered sugar
1/2 cup milk
1 tsp vanilla

Directions:
In the bowl of an electric mixer, combine the egg, sugar, milk, salt, vanilla, baking powder, and butter. Stir flour and gum together (or omit gum if your mix already includes it). Add flour mix to wet ingredients and mix into a dough. Roll dough out about 1/2 to 3/4-inch thick on a gluten free floured surface, and, using a donut cutter, cut into donut shapes. Fry in a deep fat fryer at about 365 degrees until golden brown on the bottom side. Flip, and fry again. Drain on paper towels. Whisk together a glaze with the powdered sugar, milk and vanilla. Drizzle glaze over donuts.

COMING OVER COBBLER

Ingredients:
3 pints (about 5 to 6 cups) fresh blueberries, rinsed and dried
1 cup granulated sugar
2 tsp freshly grated lemon zest
3 Tbsp gluten free flour mix

Topping Ingredients:
1 1/4 cups gluten free flour mix
6 Tbsp granulated sugar
1 1/2 tsp baking powder
1/4 tsp salt
6 Tbsp (3/4 stick) butter, chilled & cut into bits
1 egg, beaten
1 tsp vanilla extract
1 Tbsp granulated sugar
1/2 tsp ground cinnamon
1/4 tsp ground nutmeg

Directions:
Preheat oven to 375 degrees. Spray a pie plate or baking dish with non-stick cooking spray. Place blueberries into prepared baking dish. In a small bowl, combine sugar and the lemon zest. Add in the flour and whisk until thoroughly combined. Sprinkle mixture evenly over berries in prepared baking dish, stirring until well blended. Set aside. In a medium bowl, whisk together flour, sugar, baking powder and salt. Using a pastry blender or two knives, cut butter into flour mixture until it resembles coarse crumbs. In a small bowl, whisk vanilla into beaten egg using a fork. Add beaten egg and vanilla to flour mixture, stirring until moistened and dough holds together. Spread biscuit crumble topping evenly over fruit filling. Sprinkle cinnamon-sugar over all and, if desired, dust with nutmeg. Bake until topping is golden brown and filling is cooked through and bubbly, about 40 to 45 minutes. Serve with vanilla ice cream.

FRESH FRUIT TRIFLE

Ingredients:

1 gluten free yellow cake or pound cake, cut into 2-inch squares
3 to 4 cups fresh or frozen fruit
1 16-oz container frozen whipped topping (softened)

Directions:

In a glass trifle dish, layer fruit, then cake and then the whipped topping. Repeat layers until dish is full. Refrigerate until ready to serve.

EASY APPLE CRISP

Ingredients:
3 20-oz cans sliced apples (not apple pie filling)
1/3 cup packed brown sugar
2 Tbsp gluten free flour
1 tsp ground cinnamon
1/4 tsp salt
1/2 cup pecans, chopped
1 cup old-fashioned oats (make sure they are gluten free)
2 sticks butter, sliced into pats

Directions:
Preheat oven to 375 degrees. Spray a 13 x 9-inch baking dish with non-stick cooking spray. Add the apples, brown sugar, flour, cinnamon and salt. Toss to combine. Sprinkle the remaining ingredients evenly over apples. Spread the butter pats evenly around on top of the oats mixture. Bake 40 to 45 minutes or until topping is golden brown, apples are tender and juices are bubbling. Serve warm.

HONEY-VANILLA MASCARPONE PUDDING

Ingredients:

1 cup mascarpone cheese
6 oz cream cheese, very soft
1/4 cup sour cream
1/4 cup sugar
1 tsp lemon zest
1 tsp vanilla extract
1-2 Tbsp honey, warmed
4 cups mixed berries, such as raspberries, blackberries and halved strawberries
1/2-1 cup chopped pistachios
Sweetened whipped cream (optional)

Directions:

In a medium serving bowl, whisk together the mascarpone, cream cheese, sour cream, sugar, lemon zest, vanilla and honey. Refrigerate for 15 minutes before spooning into individual bowls. Spread the berries and pistachios on top of each serving and add a dollop of sweetened whipped cream, if desired. Serve with gluten free cookies.

GLUTEN FREE FRUIT PIZZA

Ingredients:
1 box gluten free sugar cookie mix
1 8-oz package cream cheese, softened
1/2 cup sugar
Fresh fruit of choice such as strawberries, blueberries, orange slices, pineapple, banana slices, kiwi slices...

Directions:
Follow instructions on box to prepare the sugar cookies and then bake the dough as one giant cookie on a pizza pan. Remove the cookie from oven and cool. Using an electric mixer, combine the cream cheese and sugar until creamy and smooth. Spread on cookie crust. Arrange fruit on top of the cream cheese and chill until ready to serve.